I AM

I AM

Poems for
Expansion & Renewal

Catherine Quiring, MA

CONTENTS

PART II

Spiritual & Systemic Expansion

AUTHOR'S NOTE

Dear Reader,

These poems have helped me navigate my own journey of healing, renewal, and expansion. Now I want to share them with you.

These words come from my soul, and I share them here in hopes that they will nourish your soul as they have mine. May these words bring richness to the soil of your inner world, light to illumine, and space to expand and breathe into the mystery and wonder of life.

Love and light,

Catherine

"As they become known to and accepted by us, our feelings and the honest exploration of them become sanctuaries and spawning grounds for the most radical and daring of ideas. They become a safe-house for that difference so necessary to change and the conceptualization of any meaningful action."

—Audre Lorde

Poems for Personal Growth & Care

I am home

I am home
I can't say I wandered far away

More like . . .
Parts of me were missing

They got
Stuffed down
Shoved in a closet
Stuck in the basement
Swallowed
Ignored
Locked outside

But now
They've been welcomed home
And I am all of me
And I am here

It is good

I have made my home inside
A place of rest
That is welcoming and abundant
Full of compassion
And curiosity
A spark of life
Connected and courageous
Creativity and laughter and dance

I looked inside my home
Inside my life
(And outside too)
And I say
It is good

I no longer have rules posted inside

I no longer have rules posted inside
. . . or anyone enforcing them.

Instead I have a table—
A round table,
An abundant table,

Where we all gather
and laugh
and share stories.

We work together,
share heartaches,
and struggles together.

We share when we annoy each other
when we're frustrated and
want something different.

We listen—
we figure out what that different is
together
so we can all be here—together.

No one left out,

no one in the shadows,
no one in the basement,
no one in the attic,

No one watching, or evaluating, or judging—
No one we have to please,
or live up to.
We're just here
. . . and it's Amazing.

I AM ME

I am me
I am me
I am me

I am

I am me—
And that is all I need to be.

I AM ME
I AM ME
I AM ME

I AM

I AM ME—
AND THAT IS ALL I NEED TO BE.

NOTE: This piece feels more like a declaration of being, than a poem *per se*. From the solid and rest-filled place of being me, there is the play on the best term I have for the divine at present, I AM—realizing the sacredness and power of being a part of and connected to the divine, enabled by fully coming home to my own being.

I lost some words

I lost some words
in order to survive.
I needed them
to be whole
But
they had to go—
would have threatened
necessary connection.
could have meant
rejection, emotional tension, despair

I lost them,
threw them away,
buried them inside.
Sometimes I forgot that they existed,
but
other times I heard . . .
their drum beat deep inside
—don't forget me, you need me,
    come back for me, I can help you—
a lost language I didn't know how
to interpret at the time.

I am finding those words again,
    reclaiming them as mine:

No

I DON'T WANT TO
    (. . . and I'm still a good person)
    I don't want to be in charge of your
        emotional well being
    I don't want to hide myself to be accepted
    I don't want to—
        and that's reason enough

I DON'T HAVE TO
    I don't have to help
    I don't have to rescue
    I don't have to make sure you feel okay
    I don't have to explain it until you
        understand and agree

My reclaimed words empower me . . .

I CAN
    I can live my own life
    I can have autonomy
    I can trust myself

I want to
I want to pay attention to things that
bring wonder
I want to let my healing flow into the world
I want to be spontaneous and silly
without fear

I choose
I choose to let you be in charge of your
own emotional response
I choose to resolve conflict, but not rescue
I choose to speak up for myself

I choose Me.

I have a guard dog inside

I have a guard dog inside
He sits
at the edges
of the door to my life
And he watches for me

He lets me know
Who is safe to let in
Who to keep at a distance

He knows it's okay to bark
And to growl

I don't have to be Nice
I don't have to be Perfect
I don't have to be Pretty

I can be me
And I can be safe

Before the dog
He was a tornado
And he held me hostage
Because he didn't think we were safe

He was a wall of protection to the outside
And a cage for the inside

But now we know each other
And we know it is safe
He has transformed into who he was made to be

We work together
My guard dog and me
He is me
And I love him

He loves that
I let him come out
And let him be him

We watch
And keep company
Together

I can know my strength

I don't fear the fall
that everything's too good
so something bad might be around the corner

there might be
there might not be

the difference is I know I can handle it
I know that I have me
and that I can deal with any pain that comes
no matter how heart wrenching

I don't have to look for it
I don't have to wait for it
I can be in me
and I can know my strength.

Have to

I have banished
the words "I have to"
from
my vocabulary.

They no longer exist for me

Instead I listen to a different rhythm,
a different flow,
a different voice:

I want to
I can
I like to

A never-ending flow and rush,
Sometimes a trickle,
Sometimes a torrent:

I like
I don't like
This is for me
This isn't for me
I can wait or I can go . . .
I have lots of choices.

Sometimes I say:
"I can only do what I can do"
and what I can do is enough.
It is enough for me
To Be
and anyone that disagrees
can disagree
With Me.

I belong

I only belong to me
I belong to me and no one else

I love and connect
I am loved and connected
But I do not belong to you
I belong only to myself

I am my own

I am my own
To know
To hold
To love

It is enough
It is more than enough

I am never not enough
For myself

I am my greatest ally
strength-She

I am whole
I am known
I am me
I am

Naked

I like my naked body
This is new to me

Being unclothed
Feeling whole
Nothing's missing

I'm whole
And full
And good

My body is my clothes
My body is me
This wonderful skin
I love to be in it

My feelings nourish me

I am in awe of my heart
How can it hold so many feelings
So many
At the same time
They jostle for attention
For space
They sit down politely
(sometimes)

They give my life fullness
Vitality
The spark of life
Fireworks exploding into the sky
In excitement
A quiet ebb of grief
Sometimes a rumble of thunder or
    earthquake of anger
But they're all there
Navigating me through this life
Helping me know what I need
Who I am

My feelings nourish me
And I release them to do their work

I planted some words inside today

> I planted some words
> inside
> today
>
> They nourished me
> Deep in the earth of my soul
>
> When they sprout, I will be glad
> Right now
> I am glad for the seeds
>
> The seeds are my words
> Coming back to me
> Full of gratitude and
> Recognition

I know the way

I know the way
In some ways, the way is
Inside
And also outside

It's more like a compass

I have a compass at my core
Pointing me
in My direction

Holding me near
Centering me
Bringing the sifted past
To point the way forward

And sending me forth like a bird in flight
Holding me up from below

As I soar overhead
I know the way
The way is inside me
And reaches before me

Coming home

I'm doing the work
The work of coming home
And the work has become easy

Because I've cleared out all of the
Shrapnel
The wounds
They've been tended to and healed

And now we are calling in
and reclaiming
all the parts that have wandered
    and are coming home
I'm so glad you're here

I'm finding myself
And knowing myself
For the first time
And every time
And before time
And this time

I am myself
And I am home

PART II

*Poems for
Spiritual & Systemic
Expansion*

Baby bird

I am like a baby bird these days
mouth wide open,
hungry,
but not for physical food.
For soul nourishment,
a new way to see.
Teach me this new way,
this new way for me
but really the Ancient Ways:
The Wisdom of
First
Peoples
and Mother Earth
and Wisdom
Herself.

My soul is malnourished
from consuming
and never being satisfied;
Striving,
and never finding the finish line,
or rest.
I am worn out

from being in the world
and not of it.

The world—this earth—
is my road home:
to belonging,
and knowing,
and connection.
Giving and receiving
the ebb and flow of
Life.

I am returning
to wonder
to my home
to myself
to my kin.

And they receive me;
but they also need healing.
They have been trampled,
and "tamed,"
depleted and consumed.

They need me as much as I need them.

I have a tree of wisdom and life

I have a tree of wisdom and life
inside me

Lush and abundant
Majestic and bold

It grew out of nothing

I cleared the ground
of shrapnel
left from the days
of unknowing—

The ground became a desert.

Then a Goddess appeared.

I did not know her name then,
Only that she came from the ground—
the ground of my life
at the core of my soul;
she sits with patience
and daring:
An invitation to live and be at rest.

As my parts gathered and played,
climbing on her weighty breasts
they knew they were home and it was safe.

I do not have to ask for anything,
I do not have to struggle.

The Tree came next—
in an instant it grew:

Antonio's magic Encanto Tree
came to life
in my core:

I sit with my back against its trunk;
I receive its support,
I receive its love,
. . . and its knowing.

I know
Divine Wisdom is inside me.
She is with me,
She watches over me,
She is me,
I am home.

My prayer is rest

It wasn't always this way

I used to pray through sweat and tears
Pleadings
Not really in my body
Always begging
Trained to be on my knees for extra power
God will be happy with you now

Now
now . . .

Now I hear the gentle breeze
running
It has nowhere to go and it is happy

I feel the solid ground beneath my feet
holding
Me
Supporting
Me
Loving me
To life

It likes that I want nothing from it

Except what it wants to give
It gives in abundance
When it is
Supported
And not
Alone

Mama wind
Strength of sun

Rain-drops like little kisses—
Sometimes soft, and sometimes much more

Witness us
Be whole with us
Be
With us

Live with us
This is prayer
Rest

I never knew I was held

I never knew I was held.
Held and supported, without exception.
Without expectations. Without strings attached.

Held by Mother Earth.
Love is actually a hard word to use,
   even though I know that to be true as well.
Love holds a fragrance of expectation to me.
The anticipation of love being returned.
Of constant connection.
Love and devotion.

To distinguish, I call love from Mother Earth
something else.
Supported,
Known,
Never alone.

. . . Never smothering,
Never expecting,
Yet never a doormat.

Always wild and free
Vibrating and flowing to its own rhythm.

Never tame or tamed . . .
Calling me
to the same.
The wildness, beauty, and freshness.
Her unbroken life force,
the beating heart of the world.

Mother Earth is from below, a part of me,
Always supporting me.
Immanence.

PART II

This is so different from the divine I was taught.
The immutable, invisible, omnipresent,
    omnipotent Father God of Heaven and Earth.
A force to be reckoned with.
A force to be feared.
More than a force—a god in the image of
    an Imperial Man.
Always saying, "not enough"—
Do more—pray more, repent more,
    evangelize more.
Always the threat of torment, of separation,
    of abandonment,
Pressing from above.

The pressure was wrapped with words of "love"
As it insisted on:
Devotion, Adoration, Worship
Without ceasing.
And demanded:
Obedience, Conformity, Compliance, Submission,
    and Self-Sacrifice.
It commanded:
Thou Shalt Not
And tried to consume, and punish,
    and shame my life-force out of me.
It tried to take me from myself,
    and replace me with itself.
In the name of "saving my soul"
    it tried to violently take it from me.
It tried to rape me, while shaming me
    for having a body.
It came to steal, and kill, and destroy,
All the while projecting this on
    the imaginary "devil."

I was "bought with a price"
    and told I should be grateful I was chosen.
I joined the harem of the sexually trafficked,
    who were told they were whores,
and deserved no better,

and must obey their Masters,
who doubled as their Lovers and Saviors.

PART III

I escaped.
And returned to Myself.
As I healed, I found life in Myself
and celebrated that Life.
I no longer had to question it,
shame myself for it,
or exile it for fear it would be crushed or stolen.
I was Myself
And I was Whole.

PART IV

After I had enough safety and courage and rest
in my wholeness,
I had space to explore, and connect again
    with the Divine.
I found I was connected with I AM
    in my wholeness, but I had no name
    for this mystery.
As time went on, a name emerged for
    the transcendent divine:
Goddess.

She is the Moon and the Planets,
the Gravity and pull of the Tides,
She whispers the Hum,
the Vibration,
the Flow
of Life—
in and around me.
I whisper back with my Breath—
the tide of life flowing into me
and through me
and out of me.
The Breath that is me—and more than me—
    at the same time.

She asks nothing of me.
I am free in her presence.

The Wisdom of Life
is simultaneously as close
and as far away as I need her to be.

Never imposing.

Always bestowing—
Self-sovereignty.

She lives in mystery

and illumination.
Cloaked in the wind . . .
and yet perfectly clear.

Goddess and Mother Earth dance together.
Shimmering Moonlight
A Frolicking Stream
Lush Honeysuckle
A Sigh of Contentment

I rest with them and receive these gifts
delivered on a breeze
lighting the way.

It is said

It is said
That God
Is
Genderless
But—must be
Called a
Man

He
His
Never deviate
Never question
God is a Man

It is not God you seek
But yourself
As Exalted Ruler
Over all
People
Animals
And Earth

But this God
Who you say must be He-Ruler

Showed Himself . . .

As a baby
Who never ruled
Who hung out with the outsiders
Disregarded the rules
Questioned the elite
Lifted up the poor
Touched wounds
And washed dirty feet

That is not ruling

That is living
And leading
And loving

God-with-us (not over us)

Expansion

why do you search for god out there?
for transcendence?

and in the process cut off the ability to see
and be a part of immanence
right here

instead you spend your time proving
and parsing
searching for a reality
for a god
beyond our knowing and our grasp

looking
learning
longing
navel-gazing
searching for reasons why you can't hear god

and all the time god is whispering
all around us
can you listen for immanence?
can you look around you at the divine
can you receive it
and restore that connection

instead of cutting yourself off
from all that is this world
in search of something else

can you receive what is here?
can you be a part of the divine here
all that is within you and around you
speaking words of freedom
and truth and life
I found a well-spring—
it's inside
the well-spring that I heard would come
    from outside, from the holy spirit
and I found it inside
I found it through the earth
through immanence
through knowing and being connected to
myself:
    trusting myself (not distrusting)
    loving myself (not second-guessing)
    knowing myself (not avoiding myself).
knowing myself is the greatest doorway to
knowing
others
and the divine

if you can't be in self
you can't be connected to anything else

all that's left is
pleading
hoping
longing
desperation . . .
for something that is already inside you
(that you were told to look for outside of you)

that empty hole
that I was told is a god-shaped hole
    that only god can fill;
it's You—
you already have it inside.
cast off the burdens
—as jesus said—
and I will give you rest.
yes, I know jesus
he's with me
he never left me

he loves that I drink of this water every day
and that it's new and fresh and renewing
and I am there too

I am the life
I am my life
I am my only life
and jesus is with me
jesus is with me in my life
jesus loves me and my life
jesus loves me the way I am
and who I am

we were made from expansion
from a tiny little seed
speck, dot
big bang if you will that kept exploding
    and expanding
in energy and colors
vibrance and life

all we do now is try to cultivate
squash it
control it
excavate it

what if we let it expand
what if we let it be reborn
what if there is more life here than we realized
and more hope for us

what if we step out of the way
and listen
then we may hear our path forward

God

The term "God" sometimes works for me
And sometimes doesn't

"God" is so laced with
The patriarchy:
A male
Ruler
In the sky

Sometimes I make the letters small
—god—
So I know she is universal
With and among
Not
Over

But really,
I like other words better
Expansive words
With and among and within me words

Words like . . .
Life
Flow
Universe

Divine She
The Divine We
Non-binary and both together
All the colors of the rainbow
Spread out we are a color wheel of beauty
Contained in One
Contained in All
Not contained at all
We are One

There is more to the story

For many years,
I followed all the rules
that Christian patriarchy gave me
wrapped in the gift wrap called "family values."
I didn't know there was another choice,
another way to see,
another path to take.

It was supposed to protect me
    and make me a holy person.
Or that's what I was told.

Instead,
it made me a shell of a person
too small and weak to protest.

And I was one of the "lucky ones"
—At least I was white,
and wanted to marry a man,
so I got applause and status for what I gave up.

Others who could never mark their purity ruler
    "white" were subjugated and oppressed
inside and out.

Land taken,
families separated,
lives ended after torture
in the name of discipline,
law and order,
god's order,
and "civilized" living.

And if your sexuality did not align—
could not,
would not,
conform
to the extreme binaries of
submissive woman
or lone ranger man,
you were shunned,
shamed,
jailed,
and denied basic human rights.

Now I know there is another way,
There is more to the story than what I was told.
I have healed and nourished myself
    back to wholeness.
I have been learning the ancient ways
    of recently bruised peoples,

and I stand with them.
I will not tolerate ideologies, worldviews,
    and laws disguised as gifts,
that are really instruments of torture, control,
    and death.

Together we rise,
We sing, we chant,
It is not the end.
We will overcome.

Heaven

I have been to
heaven,
even though
I am alive

The heaven I speak of
you see,
that heaven is
inside.

One day
as I was tending
my inner world,
healing parts
that were wounded
there,

I discovered
that
when they were
whole
and healed again,

I could see them differently
and the different

looked like—
heaven

I couldn't tell you how I knew
but I knew just the same
heaven is not when you die—
heaven is a place I found inside

It's hard to describe
this version of heaven,
but it felt like a place
where I could know myself,
be whole and alive.
A place of truth, discovery, openness,
curiosity.

Different parts of me—
different ages and roles, shapes and sizes,
walked together and talked.
We reflected on times before,
and made plans for the future.
We found honesty the cure.
Togetherness and separateness together.

The prayer

I want to go back
Really, I have gone back
inside
To tell the young girl
The me-girl
who was on her knees

Asking Jesus to come into her heart
With all the earnestness she had
(after the shock wore off
that she was told she was bad
And didn't know god after all
"You're sinful" he says
And god can't be near you
Unless you pray the prayer
I give you)

That the man that told you that—was bad
And actually, you just found out your parents
    thought so too
But they didn't tell you for some reason
They didn't tell you
they didn't like him

And he made them
uncomfortable

Why is that you wonder?
They didn't think it affected
you?
They thought it was something to Celebrate,
Even though
They didn't like

How
he
told
you
"The good news"

It was still supposedly "good news"

Really,
It feels like what happened was
You stopped . . .
Listening
To
Yourself

You
Started . . .

Managing
Yourself

You only listened to
The
Words
The church
Told you

The Way
The Truth
The Life
They say—we know the way—only this way!

A certain way
To read
The bible

A certain way
To hear God
To know God
To talk about God

You had to live according to those ways
Make sure
God
Was on

Your side
And close to you
At all times

It was hard
It was a lot of pressure

And it didn't have anything to do with god

The Divine was in you all the time
The Divine Feminine no one spoke of
The Goddess
Who has been excluded
She is you
She knows you
She speaks your name

Now I know
My heart was always hers
Because it's Mine

The all-of-us divine

God-with-us
Is genderfull,
not genderless
She-He-They-We God
A fluid motion
Through time
and space
An open rainbow
Expansive and alive
The All-of-Us Divine

Prayer is not a transaction

Prayer is not a transaction:
Something I
Ask for,
Plead for,
Beg for,

And wait for an answer . . .

I wonder will I ever get one?

Maybe . . .
if I see the outcome I wanted
Or maybe I see nothing.

And then my faith in god is dependent on that,
my hope for what happens is dependent on that

Sending it out into the netherworld
to a god that I've been told is a certain way
but not because
I've experienced god that way, but
just because I've been told god is that way

It's a very strange way to relate.
We're told it's not supposed to be a transaction

but how can it be otherwise?
How can we actually listen (and hear something)
in the way we're told to listen?
We're supposed to listen for a still small voice,
an inner resonance
but what if we don't have that, what then?

And if we have too much
Voice
then we're called crazy
and filled with a demon;
seeing visions is hallucinating,
you can't trust dreams
But you can trust "the Words of God"
    as we give them to you . . .
Then who am I listening to?
You
Or god?

How is anyone supposed to see or hear
    or know god
in such a rigid, small way?

My prayer is not
a transaction
anymore.

My prayer is my life
my prayer is me
Being
in the world
and listening
to the wave
and the particle

Seeing the different ways
one scene
looks
in a different light

Seeing the
Moon
and the stars;
The moon's courses
change and shift

Inside—
and on the Shore,
Holding me . . .
to the Earth
Holding me . . .
and gently swaying
Rocking me like a mother rocks

her children
and also standing
Still
A great foundation
that never moved
beneath the weight of my body
resting, playing, loving, living

Prayer is not a transaction.
Prayer is life
Prayer is breath
Prayer is me
in Life.

The spring of wonder

I wonder a lot
Have you noticed?

This wondering
Has unlocked a vast reservoir in me
Like finding a spring
No one knew
Was there

Never-ending water
Trickling sometimes,
Gushing others
But always refreshing

I am a stream
I am a spring
I am my wonder
And my wonder gives me life

Purity

Purity drained me of my life.
A siphon of all that was delicious, and sensual,
    and dark, and deep.

A digging out, an excavation, of the earth of my life.
    The rich soil dumped out in the dump
    where it could not nurture me or any other life.

A hollowing out of all imagination,
    replaced with the concrete of linear thought,
the dogmas that were taught,
the rational and right way to think
and to be.

The dark internal caverns full of mystery and magic
Were roped off, barricaded, and neglected.
They existed for me only in passing wisps of
memory—
even then they were relegated and retaught:
    must be a dangerous myth, don't even think it,
let alone go there.

Once Purity had emptied me,
it transformed into
a ruler to judge me by,

which must be examined and marked at every
moment—
an introspective micro-managing,
I asked myself every moment:
Am I Christian enough?
Sold-out enough?
Am I . . .
Pure of heart?
Pure of thought?

Do I have pure motives?
Am I doing everything for God?
Doing what Jesus would do?
Honoring my parents?
Taking captive every thought?
Keeping my temple pure?
Eradicating my sexuality?
Warding off every temptation?

If the answer was yes, I passed—
and I had . . .
the relief of a moment
the reward of a gold star,
the title of the golden child,
and the assurance of my identity as a sheep
    entering the Kingdom of Heaven.

If the answer was no, I failed—
and I found instead . . .
guilt and shame, conviction and repentance,
    fear of backsliding and falling away
    if it continued (will I miss the Rapture?),
    fear of God's displeasure, fear of myself,
    inner judgment for not having enough discipline,
    fear that I might be identified as a goat
    and sent away from the Kingdom.

After years of this,
I was left a wisp of a person,
No substance to draw from.
Only the shell of a rigid statue left,
Hollow inside.

I can't do it all

"I can't do it all!"—she cried out overwhelmed.
It's too much for me.
I'm spent.
I'm through.
I throw in the towel.
I don't want to try.
I've already failed too many times.

My kids need to eat,
The house is a pig-sty . . .
I can't lie in bed binging TV,
Hoping someone will come
and rescue me.

My mind won't be quiet,
And my body is through.
What oh, what is a girl to do?

I want to be Mom-Hero and do it all,
But my body says no—
It's too much to bear . . .

The expectations are too great for one person
I say.
I'm too depleted to save the day.

PART II

This overwhelm is not my doom
It is my wake-up call to . . .
shake off and unburden
myself of the lie:
this idealized version
of American life.

It does not feel like utopia to me
but I burden I bear
—unseen—
daily.

The invisible labor of Wives,
Mothers, and Lovers,
is the unseen foundation
of our
patriarchal nation.

We are crushed to form
a male-centric vision
of the good life:

The utopian nuclear family.

    Never in want,
    Always well-clothed
    Politeness and smiles,
    Always on time.

    Be thrifty,
    Yet give me abundance.
    Give me a house-full of kids
    ——who are always quiet.

I would rather be Real
and fully myself,
free of the pressures
to please and do more—
This is the life
I have in store.

This is the family I can create:
One that is authentic,
but sometimes late.
We show up with heart,
with compassion for others;
No perfection expected—
from you or from me.

I may be messy—and tired sometimes,
but I'm full of love
and presence,
in the house—
not a foundation
hidden below ground.

Together we are creating a new order
of what's really important.
Acceptance, autonomy,
delight in each other.
Instead of an injunction to do it all—
Freedom to be
To love
To know
—and be known
this is the life I claim as my own.

The goddeses of enough

I went to meet
some parts of mine
in my inner world—
To talk about scarcity
and abundance.

I found that four goddesses appeared
along with my four parts.
I didn't expect them.
I was looking for burdens to uncover
and release
And instead I found the goddesses.
They became four orbs of light
like moons in orbit. Connected
in their patterns.
Geometric reciprocity.
A dance in the night sky
inside my life.
Luminous love
and generosity
lighting my way.

I don't have words and labels to describe them.
And I get the feeling

that they like it that way.
They are mysteriously enough.
Labeling them makes them a subject,
    an object to understand.
Knowing in mystery—
this is the thing!
Ironically enough, the only way
to be in relationship with the divine,
to know them fully for who they are.

Not distancing myself from them,
retreating from my body into my mind,
and dissecting their importance.

I am with them.
They are a gift.
The gift of nascent presence,
Softly glowing enough-ness.

The parts I met at the onset
were astonished
and relieved.
They had been kindly and tenaciously
fielding the feelings of scarcity and abundance.
Trying always to evoke abundance in a world
that says "more, more, more"

But when you get more, your ability to buy more
    diminishes as the money has been spent.
And to get more, you must deplete other
    valuable resources—your time and energy.
There is always scarcity on some front
    in a consuming system.
They were afraid of scarcity, of feeling deprived,
    but didn't know the solution.
They managed and loved me the best they could.

They are thankful to have the goddesses
    to relieve them
of their never-ending, circular patterns to possess
    and feel whole.

They are resting and learning,
    watching as the goddesses teach . . .

A giving system where none feels excluded—
no more fear that one part will steal from another
    to meet its needs

(I acknowledge the harm that I have done to you.
    I will not take from you energy
    or from you time anymore.
    I will ask for your teamwork to meet a need.

We will no longer be taskmasters or consumers
    to blindly attempt to fill ourselves up.)

We are learning the gift of reciprocity, of generosity.
A willingness to share when there is less
    and help each other through.

Motivation and attention, can you learn new ways
    with us to not fall into a hole
    and stop when there is lack?

You know how to pivot and keep moving around
    rocks and obstacles, like an effervescent stream.

And maybe sometimes we need a new way.
    Let us ask the goddesses.

Weeds

I was looking at my garden
And wondering
What do I do with the weeds?

I want to let them live
Those plucky things
Wild and free
With beautiful flowers
And divergent leaves

I just don't like how they strangle
What we try to plant
And cultivate

But is that our fault
Or theirs?

I love how the weeds are so . . .
Tenacious
Persistent
They come back
They don't care if anyone wants them or not
They show their heads anyway
Always looking to the sun

Looking for more
Looking to be
They stretch themselves
To expand

I love the weeds
The weeds are me

I think of my kids
I don't want them Over-cultivated, Tamed,
—and I definitely don't want them Broken.

How do we grow strong weeds
A mix of the pluck and tenacity and wildness
    of the weeds
And also
The majesty and the grandeur
    of the towering trees

How do we bring these together?
In the dirt and the earth,
Make space for all of us?

Those that like to be carefully curated
    and cultivated
And those that like to be wild and free

How do we dance together
In this soil, in this earth

These things I wonder
When I look at the weeds

This is my life

I am of my emotions
They were cut off early—only good ones allowed—
I grew rigid and bright.
With a smile plastered on my face.
Only emotions allowed, only emotions allowed I say are:
Happiness, gratitude, worshipfulness, willpower,
      determination, productivity, helpfulness . . .
      wait we are all out of emotions.
Most of these aren't even feelings.

We have become numb to the rest. A ball of anxiety,
      the product of
Productiveness.
Rightness.
Do the right thing-ness.
Everything for god-ness.

Enough!
Something must change.
Treat me with kindness, listen to me, support me.
Stop using me and abusing me.
Love me.
I love you.
You are my life.

I welcome you . . .
Sweet bitterness and anger
Longing and belly-deep laughter
The swelling of my heart

They become a swell of vibration, of life,
    of understanding
. . . of experience.

Slow and quiet
Comforting and soft.
A fierce growl
—stay away.
A thrill of inspiration.
A lightning bolt of recognition.
A bittersweet sadness that comforts
    even in the pain.
Like dark chocolate
Or red wine. Warm and full, bitter and inviting.

I am of my body
My body is multi-layered,
amazing in its complexity.
Skin, muscles, bones, organs, and more
work seamlessly together to sustain my living.

I am learning that when we are cut off from
    our bodies, they can't get through to us
    with whispers, so they begin to rumble and
    shout, and break down—all in an attempt
    to get our attention.
They whisper, they scream, they shout,
    they writhe . . .

Enough!
Something must change.
Treat me with kindness, listen to me, support me.
Stop using me and abusing me.
I am not a thing, but your very life.
Love me.
I love you.
You are my life.

I welcome you . . .
Supple, lithe, full body
Sometimes muscle, sometimes softness
Full of life

Deep breaths welcomed
Down to my root
I am alive
I am me

I am my body
(and She is me)

I AM OF THE EARTH
I can hear its whispers, its beauty, its longings.
I love the rustle of the leaves teased by the wind
The song of a bird floating on the breeze
The strength of a tree rooting down
     and reaching out its lush branches
The little wildflower with its nose to the sun

I can also hear its groans, its pain, its depletion
It's enough-ness withering away

"I am life itself

"Holding, nurturing
breathing dirt and sweet water
into a never-ending cycle of life and death
     and resurrection

"I tried to speak . . .
In whispers of beauty
In lavish abundance
. . . of shade
And food.

"Until you stopped me
Cut me down
Cut me off—

"I cried out in pain
at shattered earth,
heart split by metal,
the life I nurtured felled and silent and numb
a ravaged waste
starving for something to drink.

"But you just took and took
And took some more
Thanking the god of the sky and despising me.
I am tired, but still I rise
To tell you again, louder and louder:

"Enough!
Something must change.
Treat me with kindness, listen to me,
    support and respect me.
Stop using me and abusing me.
I still love you.
Love me.
I am your life.

"I was always expanding
Rebirthing and renewing
Composting and regenerating
I will do it again, with or without you.
I would like to do it with you.
Will you choose me too?"

May the earth's groans be the groans of childbirth
Of a new beginning, not the end
A new womb of Eden
The birth of a world
New to the touch
Reverent
Alive

Speaking life to all its inhabitants
And we speak back
We love you
We honor you

We are of the earth
And the earth is with us.

I AM OF THE WATER
The water is my mother.
I ride on her back

Winding on the currents she creates,
She is my guide.

She teaches me large swells of power
And quiet ebbs,
The ever-present flow of life,

Quenching my thirst
Pure
Rushing
Strong
Good
Full
Free

Always refreshing
Never tame

She teaches me reciprocity,
the dance of interdependence:
She receives from the sky above,
which refreshes and fills her.
And she quietly nourishes the dirt below,
with her liquid love.

The water's natural flow has been taken.
She is not able to nourish as she knows how to do.

She is harnessed and glutted in some places
and rarely seen in others.

And she rises up and cries:

"Enough!
Something must change.
Treat me with kindness, listen to me,
    support and respect me.
Stop using me and abusing me.
I still love you.
Love me.
I am your life."

I AM OF THE SKY
I wander through the effervescence,
The vast expanse of sky
——-limitless, boundless, never-end-reaching
always more, always farther than I can see,
an abundance of spaciousness and nearness
Reaching beyond . . .
until it touches the star-studded cosmos,
then gravitating below . . .
until it kisses the earth.

The sky teaches me
of lightness and gravity wrapped into one.

An invisible color you cannot grab with your hands,
but can see from afar.
The movement of particles too small to perceive
yet all around and touching me.
Still at times, and rushing at others—
     as the wind joins in
to the sky's glad reality.

The sky groans and complains of the weight
     it must carry
of particles weighed by pollution,
yet trying to bring
clear breathing and clear sight again.

"Enough!
Something must change.
Treat me with kindness, listen to me,
     support and respect me.
Stop using me and abusing me.
I still love you.
Love me.
I am your life."

I AM OF THE FIRE
I see the burning light
within and without—
Passion & Intensity

Comfort & Warmth
Daring & Courage
Flicker & Spark

It draws me in
yet keeps its boundaries.
A Holy Autonomy.
Self-determination & Self-sovereignty
at its core.

"I am necessary for life,"
Fire speaks.
"I do not exist to burn, hurt, or consume
but if you get too close,
my essence will allow nothing else.

"Draw close for light and warmth,
but do not use me to destroy,"
the fire warns.

"Enough!
Something must change.
Treat me with kindness, listen to me,
    support and respect me.
Stop using me and abusing me.
I still love you.

Love me.
I am your life."

This is my life
I am part of
A Great Tapestry—
Never Alone
An intricate system
of Care
and Knowing.
Earth, Water, Sky, and Fire
all with me and around me.
I learn from them and live with them.
My body and my feelings accompany me
and join my thoughts in the essence of who I am.
They help me navigate the mystery and wonder
    of Life.

Ready

It was time
I jumped off

The exhilaration was wonderful.
Fully me in my body, immersed in sky—
Held—in the moment where momentum meets
gravity—the stillness of air-held body
A miracle of a moment: not floating, not falling,
not flailing, but held.
Held in air's strong arms
Not weightless, not lighter than air, but . . .
Weighty.
The fullness of a body full of fire, and land, and
water, and sky
Full of mystery and passion, life and vibrancy . . .

Present and alive—
Senses sharpened,
I arrived.
I landed like a panther,
Lithe and ready:
Ready to wait,
Ready for action,
Ready for me,
Ready for life.

Sacred you

You're making a new life for yourself.
You're learning to find your core self,
your seat of intuition,
your inner knowing
. . . and listen to it.

Not: listen to obey, to submit, or to conform—like
you were taught.

This time the listening is different.
It's being still to remember who you are,
to release and to reclaim,
to reconnect to
sacred
you.

It's expansive, freeing,
soul-magnifying,
grounding,
earthing and unearthing,
learning and unlearning,
being
sacred
you.

ABOUT THE AUTHOR

CATHERINE QUIRING, MA, is a Licensed Mental Health Counselor and Self-Trust Coach. She specializes in helping exvangelicals learn to trust their desires and reconnect to their inner wisdom. She also helps people-pleasers learn to trust themselves and recenter themselves at the helm of their lives.

Catherine loves this life-changing work of therapy and healing and feels so privileged that she gets to spend her days doing this.

She is a cis-gendered, white, able-bodied, thin, neurodivergent female in a heteronormative relationship. She is a reformed people-pleaser and exvangelical. She is an advocate for intersectional anti-oppressive work.

Outside of work, she is an avid podcast-listener, book lover, paddleboard enthusiast, and toddler-chaser.

Connect with Catherine:
www.cqcounseling.com

Listen to the author read her poetry to you:
cqcounseling.com/i-am-audio